Love Thy Neighbor

(The Christian Purist Bible)

BY CHUN KI

Order this book online at www.trafford.com
or email orders@trafford.com

Most Trafford titles are also available at major online book retailers.

National Library of Canada Cataloguing in Publication Data

Ki, Chun, 1972-
        Love thy neighbor / Chun Ki ; B. Cantollas, front cover
artist, E.A. Wade, back cover artist.

BJ1581.2.K46 2003   158.1   C2003-903024-5

Printed in the United States of America.

ISBN: 978-1-4120-0357-5 (sc)

*Our mission is to efficiently provide the world's finest, most comprehensive book publishing
service, enabling every author to experience success. To find out how to publish your book,
your way, and have it available worldwide, visit us online at www.trafford.com*

Trafford rev. 11/01/2010

Trafford
PUBLISHING®   www.trafford.com

North America & international
toll-free: 1 888 232 4444 (USA & Canada)
phone: 250 383 6864 ♦ fax: 812 355 4082

"My only crime is that I love too much . . . ."

GHIN KI CIRCA 1998 C.E.

In loving memory of Sheila, whose thought provoking statements helped to open my soul's awareness and to my loving family whose spiritual, religious, and moral examples I will always cherish . . .

I. I am. That's what God answered Moses upon their initial encounter in the Old Testament, and my humble belief in that prophetic self evaluation is what brings you, my friend, with me back to the year 1997 C. E., 300 miles north of Beijing, on the Great Wall of China. It was my first and last encounter with the wise, yet mysterious and elusive Chun Ki, a so-called, self-proclaimed Christian Purist. This chance meeting took place on a misty afternoon as I strayed away from my methodical tour group and was perusing from one vacated guard tower to another, when I happened to bump into a peculiar-looking stranger with Asian features coming towards me, hurriedly, from the opposite direction.

"Hey! Help!" The force of our accidental collision nearly knocked me off the rain slick precipice and down into the foggy, deep, and snowy northern Chinese countryside. Our whimsical tour guide had just informed us that the surrounding hillsides were notorious for hosting a variety of wolf packs that patrol its vacated length throughout the frigid Manchurian nights. Now, as I began to lose my footing and started mumbling the Lord's Prayer, the mysterious stranger's robed arm lashed out and hooked my forearm at the last possible second. Then, in President's English, he queried, "Hello brother, I, I am, I am Chun Ki, and I have chosen to help you, because I just like to help, but first, you must answer me this, if you can honestly answer me, truly, this one question I have in mind?" Of course, me being overwhelmed by my nearness and closeness to my Earthly fate and intrigued by this fascinating and thoughtful pattern of inquiry from this helpful stranger, I, with newfound hope responded, "OK, my friend, but what if I answer incorrectly?"

To which he responded, "There is no right or wrong answer for you, me, or mankind, if it comes truly from your heart, for there is only one judge. So, my friend, what is your personal definition of the meaning of life?" So I, being a non-denominational Christian in belief at the time answered, "To be happy." And with my shallow, but spontaneous answer, the bemused stranger, Chun Ki, pulled me up on my feet and chuckled, "Well done. It was not in my nature to have let you fall, regardless, if I could help it, but it is refreshing to know that at least you have pondered one of the eternal questions of mankind. But that is only the beginning my brother, for my time on Earth, and particularly on this Great Wall, grows short. I am in transit, and have a message to give to you for the lost of this world, if your faith proves strong enough?"

Then, Chun Ki inquired, "And to which God, or Creator, might I humbly ask, were you just praying to?" To which I replied, "The Christian God" at which he chuckled and replied, "Really, well, I'm a Christian purist, and live purely by the words of Christ alone from the book of Matthew, the original book from which the following three in the traditional Bible canon were derived from. Because the creation of life, or life force, may not be limited to Earth, Christ rarely specified that which mankind assumes, and oh, always remember that it's blasphemous to put words in Christ's mouth, yes, but I'm rambling my brother, my apologies. And I pray to our Creator, whom you and I choose to call God, and whom all that believe and feel God's life-force or love which flows through all living things and believe that Christ was God's son and died for the sins of mankind, negating the Old Testament teachings and making his, and only his, teachings and scriptures the living Word of God for true Christians. Then we who follow this, and his teachings alone, not the interpretations, addendums, afterthoughts, editorials, or media personalities under any name, past, present and future, and we who read Christ's Word on our own, and live it by example, are the Christian purists.

It's so simple my brother, it's hard, and so I'll say it again. CHRIST'S WORDS ARE ALL THAT MATTERS AND ALL I BELIEVE IN, NO ONE ELSE'S WORDS, I ONLY SERVE ONE MASTER, NOT MAN-MADE DOCTRINES, DEMAGOGUES, SYMBOLS AND TRADITIONS, THAT IS JUST ART, AND ONLY THROUGH CHRIST'S WORDS AND LOVE WILL I FIND MY SALVATION. JUST AS HE WALKED AMONGST US, SPOKE, AND TAUGHT TO ALL MANKIND, DO YOU NOT BELIEVE WHAT HE SAID, ARE YOU LISTENING TO ME BROTHER?" as he took my shoulders and shook me in a convicting manner.

Well, this revelation and personal testimony had taken me aback some, since, in the grand scheme of things, I had never really considered where my disillusionment with the traditional Church had irreversibly begun. I guess it all began when I started to become more inquisitive in my early adolescence about traditional doctrines followed unquestioningly by adults I loved and respected. And I began asking traditional Protestant Church elders some questions about why were, how, and who came up with these practices, our Church doctrine? Especially things that Christ hadn't even mentioned, nevertheless any of the other various contributors to the traditional Bible canon, while other things that Christ had emphasized and said to follow weren't included or taught on a regular basis. Innocently, I would pose questions such as, "Were any of Christ's teachings less relevant than others and who made that decision if it was not Christ himself to place these extra doctrines alongside Christ's own?" Other questions followed such as who had developed their particular doctrine, and did that make these extra doctrines sacred? And since they have provided their respective worshippers all of the spiritual and secular answers, then what did they think Christ would have to say about them filling in the blanks for him? Or did the respective Church founders just develop their custom made solutions on their own without consulting the traditional Bible canon for their own personal reasons? And has that style of making doctrines purely from mankind's views always been acceptable?

Well, needless to say, I wasn't the most popular youth in Sunday Schools district-wide, and, because of the unanswered questions, I eventually drifted away from the traditional Christian church as a whole. None of them proved to totally focus only on Christ's teachings, and the ones that claimed they had all the answers to their parishioners, had in fact custom designed their respective denomination's answers about the rest of mankind's eternal questions about life and God always, without the consent, but on the behalf, of Christ. I will always pray for the spiritual leaders, and they they're not intentionally hurting their parishioners, but their train of false and motley teachings, if followed, will never save the souls of their congregations, nor bring paradise on Earth during anyone's lifetime. So, after many religious question and answer sessions, I would finally end up thinking to myself, "Thanks but no thanks minister, I can be lead astray more from the words of Christ reading and practicing on my own then in your respective congregation" and walk away.

As I continued my research in my own personal quest for the true teachings of Christ and all manifestations of God, the Creator, on Earth throughout history, I began my journey, in classes, traveling, and studying literature of all types, about all of the world's religions. But as I studied the religions in a spiritual light and as historical documents, even in the modern major world religions of where God may have revealed itself in other forms, there were erected by the spiritual leaders major barriers of miscommunication, misinformation, and dilution of the universal message of love. This has contributed to leaving billions of our fellow brothers and sisters in perpetual darkness from millennia past to the present day.

I observed that these misguided spiritual leaders understand that most of the Majority don't like to read scriptures on their own volition, and would rather have their salvation fed to them, or re-written, on a silver spoon or from a pulpit rather than obtained through their own personal effort and learning methods. But life itself, and the free will given to us, never makes our personal salvation that easy.

From my conversations with believers in reincarnation with whom I have debated often, I would quote that since the number of human beings has increased phenomenally, but not as fast as the number of animal species being eradicated on Earth throughout time, then where are all the extra souls being held that don't have animal or human bodies to be born into, hmm . . .

And to some of the Muslims with whom I share casual religious literature debates with from time to time, they would inform me that they accept that Christ was a prophet, but nothing more (not the Son of God, resurrection, etc . . .), and that Mohamed was the greatest prophet, so everything else Christ said, they claimed is true, except for his claim of being the Son of God was false. Well, using their premise, I would respond, "Well if everything else Christ said was true, according to you, and Christ mentioned that John the Baptist was the last prophet, hmm . . ." To which my Muslims friends would nicely warn me to leave that point alone and walk away.

Whoops, I got away from my dialogue with Chun Ki, so I answered him with a resounding "YES!" It was all made so clear to me at that instant, that this was the point my life had led up to, despite all of the attempted brainwashing, distractions, trials, and temptations throughout my upbringing. I was finally ready to attempt to live and accept this divine clarity and truth from this wonderful stranger who had saved my life, mentally, physically, emotionally, and spiritually.

And, simultaneously, he had been transfigured spiritually in front of my eyes, into my true spiritual brother, as all peoples are to me now, no matter what faith they choose to follow, or how God may have chose to manifest itself unto them, even though Christ is, for me, the way and my connection to our Creator.

This book, "Love Thy Neighbor" is a personal testimony with the teachings and life of Christ from the earliest historical accounts, and some of the philosophies of Chun Ki based off of his worldwide wanderings, observations, and way of life as given to me by him that misty afternoon. Let it help assist the reader to a happier, fuller, more understanding, and more accepting lifestyle with our brothers and sisters in mankind through your actions and improve your personal relationship with God.

While I was catching my breath, Chun Ki looked over his shoulder, and hurriedly handed me 2 documents. Then, he whispered in my ear, "God be with you always my brother, please publish the uncorruptable and universal message of Christ alone", and scampered down the moss filled steps into the Manchurian hillside as the sun began to set on the beginning of the rest of my life's journey. That was the last I saw or heard of Chun Ki, and following this prologue I present the Christian Purist Bible (earliest account of Christ's teachings), and, as a special bonus treat, "Chunkilogy", the second document handed to me, an addendum of some of Chun Ki's philosophies, plus glossary, that will help the open-minded reader or person interested in Christian Purism to understand the universe that we live in, what is going on, how to cope with the nonsense mankind has created to dampen your full personal spiritual development, and put everything into an enlightened perspective while keeping a Christian purist frame of mind, like our brother Chun Ki. Blessings and unconditional love always!

LOVE 1

JESUS IS BAPTIZED

"Leave it like this for the time being; it is fitting that we should, in this way, do all that uprightness demands."

And when Jesus had been baptized he at once came up from the water, and suddenly the heavens opened and he saw the Spirit of God descending like a dove and coming down on him.

And suddenly there was a voice from heaven, "This is my Son, the Beloved; my favor rests on him."

TESTING IN THE DESERT

"Human beings live not on bread alone but on every word that comes from the mouth of God."

"Do not put the Lord your God to the test."

"Away with you, Satan! For scripture says: The Lord your God is the one to whom you must do homage, him alone you must serve."

"Repent, for the kingdom of Heaven is close at hand."

"Come after me and I will make you fishers of people."

THE SERMON ON THE MOUNT

How blessed are the poor in spirit: the kingdom of Heaven is theirs.

Blessed are the gentle: they shall have the earth as inheritance.

Blessed are those who mourn: they shall be comforted.

Blessed are those who hunger and thirst for uprightness: they shall have their fill.

Blessed are the merciful: they shall have mercy shown them.

Blessed are the pure in heart: they shall see God.

Blessed are the peacemakers: they shall be recognized as children of God.

Blessed are those who are persecuted in the cause of uprightness: the kingdom of Heaven is theirs.

Blessed are you when people abuse you and persecute you and speak all kinds of calumny against you falsely on my account.

Rejoice and be glad, for your reward will be great in heaven; this is how they persecuted the prophets before you.

Salt for the earth and light for the world

`You are salt for the earth. But if salt loses its taste, what can make it salty again? It is good for nothing, and can only be thrown out to be trampled under people's feet.

`You are light for the world. A city built on a hilltop cannot be hidden.

No one lights a lamp to put it under a tub; they put it on the lamp-stand where it shines for everyone in the house.

In the same way your light must shine in people's sight, so that, seeing your good works, they may give praise to your Father in heaven.

Do not imagine that I have come to abolish the Law or the Prophets. I have come not to abolish but to complete them.

In truth I tell you, till heaven and earth disappear, not one dot, not one little stroke, is to disappear from the Law until all its purpose is achieved.

Therefore, anyone who infringes even one of the least of these commandments and teaches others to do the same will be considered the least in the kingdom of Heaven; but the person who keeps them and teaches them will be considered great in the kingdom of Heaven.

`For I tell you, if your uprightness does not surpass that of the scribes and Pharisees, you will never get into the kingdom of Heaven.

`You have heard how it was said to our ancestors, you shall not kill; and if anyone does kill he must answer for it before the court.

But I say this to you, anyone who is angry with a brother will answer for it before the court; anyone who calls a brother `Fool' will answer for it before the Sanhedrin; and anyone who calls him `Traitor' will answer for it in hell fire.

So then, if you are bringing your offering to the altar and there remember that your brother has something against you,

Leave your offering there before the altar, go and be reconciled with your brother first, and then come back and present your offering.

Come to terms with your opponent in good time while you are still on the way to the court with him, or he may hand you over to the judge and the judge to the officer, and you will be thrown into prison.

In truth I tell you, you will not get out till you have paid the last penny.

`You have heard how it was said, you shall not commit adultery.

But I say this to you, if a man looks at a woman lustfully; he has already committed adultery with her in his heart.

If your right eye should be your downfall, tear it out and throw it away; for it will do you less harm to lose one part of yourself than to have your whole body thrown into hell.

And if your right hand should be your downfall, cut it off and throw it away; for it will do you less harm to lose one part of yourself than to have your whole body go to hell.

`It has also been said; Anyone who divorces his wife must give her a writ of dismissal.

But I say this to you, everyone who divorces his wife, except for the case of an illicit marriage, makes her an adulteress; and anyone who marries a divorced woman commits adultery.

But I say this to you; do not swear at all, either by heaven, since that is God's throne;

Or by earth, since that is his footstool; or by Jerusalem, since that is the city of the great King.

Do not swear by your own head either, since you cannot turn a single hair white or black.

All you need say is `Yes' if you mean yes, `No' if you mean no; anything more than this comes from the Evil One.

`You have heard how it was said: Eye for eye and tooth for tooth.

But I say this to you: offer no resistance to the wicked. On the contrary, if anyone hits you on the right cheek, offer him the other as well;

If someone wishes to go to law with you to get your tunic, let him have your cloak as well.

And if anyone requires you to go one mile, go two miles with him.

Give to anyone who asks you, and if anyone wants to borrow, do not turn away.

`You have heard how it was said; You will love your neighbor and hate your enemy.

But I say this to you, love your enemies and pray for those who persecute you;

So that you may be children of your Father in heaven, for he causes his sun to rise on the bad as well as the good, and sends down rain to fall on the upright and the wicked alike.

For if you love those who love you, what reward will you get? Do not even the tax collectors do as much?

And if you save your greetings for your brothers, are you doing anything exceptional?
Do not even the gentiles do as much? You must therefore be perfect, just as your heavenly Father is perfect."

`Be careful not to parade your uprightness in public to attract attention; otherwise you will lose all reward from your Father in heaven.

So when you give alms, do not have it trumpeted before you; this is what the hypocrites do in the synagogues and in the streets to win human admiration. In truth I tell you, they have had their reward.

But when you give alms, your left hand must not know what your right is doing;

Your almsgiving must be secret, and your Father who sees all that is done in secret will reward you.

`And when you pray, do not imitate the hypocrites: they love to say their prayers standing up in the synagogues and at the street corners for people to see them. In truth I tell you, they have had their reward.

But when you pray, go to your private room, shut yourself in, and so pray to your Father who is in that secret place, and your Father who sees all that is done in secret will reward you.

`In your prayers do not babble as the gentiles do, for they think that by using many words they will make themselves heard.

Do not be like them; your Father knows what you need before you ask him.

So you should pray like this:
Our Father in heaven,
may your name be held holy,
your kingdom come,
your will be done,
on earth as in heaven.
Give us today our daily bread.
And forgive us our debts,
as we have forgiven those who are in debt to us.

And do not put us to the test, but save us from the Evil One.

'Yes, if you forgive others their failings, your heavenly Father will forgive you yours;

But if you do not forgive others, your Father will not forgive your failings either.

'When you are fasting, do not put on a gloomy look as the hypocrites do: they go about looking unsightly to let people know they are fasting. In truth I tell you, they have had their reward.

But when you fast, put scent on your head and wash your face,

So that no one will know you are fasting except your Father who sees all that is done in secret; and your Father who sees all that is done in secret will reward you.

'Do not store up treasures for yourselves on earth, where moth and woodworm destroy them and thieves can break in and steal.

But store up treasures for yourselves in heaven, where neither moth nor woodworm destroys them and thieves cannot break in and steal.

For wherever your treasure is, there will your heart be too.

'The lamp of the body is the eye. It follows that if your eye is clear, your whole body will be filled with light.

But if your eye is diseased, your whole body will be darkness. If then, the light inside you is darkened, what darkness that will be!

'No one can be the slave of two masters: he will either hate the first and love the second, or be attached to the first and despise the second. You cannot be the slave both of God and of money.

'That is why I am telling you not to worry about your life and what you are to eat, nor about your body and what you are to wear. Surely life is more than food, and the body more than clothing!

Look at the birds in the sky. They do not sow or reap or gather into barns; yet your heavenly Father feeds them. Are you not worth much more than they are?

Can any of you, however much you worry, add one single cubit to your span of life?

And why worry about clothing? Think of the flowers growing in the fields; they never have to work or spin;

Yet I assure you that not even Solomon in all his royal robes was clothed like one of these.

Now if that is how God clothes the wild flowers growing in the field which are there today and thrown into the furnace tomorrow, will he not much more look after you, you who have so little faith?

So do not worry; do not say, 'What are we to eat? What are we to drink? What are we to wear?'

It is the gentiles who set their hearts on all these things. Your heavenly Father knows you need them all.

Set your hearts on his kingdom first, and on God's saving justice, and all these other things will be given you as well.

So do not worry about tomorrow: tomorrow will take care of itself. Each day has enough trouble of its own."

DO NOT JUDGE

`Do not judge, and you will not be judged;

Because the judgements you give are the judgements you will get, and the standard you give are the judgements you will get, and the standard you use will be the standard used for you.

Why do you observe the splinter in your brother's eye and never notice the great log in your own?

And how dare you say to your brother, `Let me take that splinter out of your eye,' when, look, there is a great log in your own?

Hypocrite! Take the log out of your own eye first, and then you will see clearly enough to take the splinter out of your brother's eye.

`Do not give dogs what is holy; and do not throw your pearls in front of pigs, or they may trample them and then turn on you and tear you to pieces.

`Ask, and it will be given to you; search, and you will find; knock, and the door will be opened to you.

Everyone who asks receives; everyone who searches finds; everyone who knocks will have the door opened.

Is there anyone among you who would hand his son a stone when he asked for bread?

Or would hand him a snake when he asked for a fish?

If you, then, evil as you are, know how to give your children what is good, how much more will your Father in heaven give good things to those who ask him!

`So always treat others as you would like them to treat you; that is the Law and the Prophets.

`Enter by the narrow gate, since the road that leads to destruction is wide and spacious, and many take it;

But it is a narrow gate and a hard road that leads to life, and only a few find it.

`Beware of false prophets who come to you disguised as sheep but underneath are ravenous wolves.

You will be able to tell them by their fruits. Can people pick grapes from thorns, or figs from thistles?

In the same way, a sound tree produces good fruit but a rotten tree bad fruit.

A sound tree cannot bear bad fruit, nor a rotten tree bear good fruit.

Any tree that does not produce good fruit is cut down and thrown on the fire.

I repeat, you will be able to tell them by their fruits.

It is not anyone who says to me, 'Lord, Lord,' who will enter the kingdom of Heaven, but the person who does the will of my Father in heaven.

When the day comes many will say to me, 'Lord, Lord, did we not prophesy in your name, drive out demons in your name, work many miracles in your name?'

Then I shall tell them to their faces: I have never known you; away from me, all evildoers!

'Therefore, everyone who listens to these words of mine and acts on them will be like a sensible man who built his house on rock.

Rain came down, floods rose, gales blew and hurled themselves against that house, and it did not fall: it was founded on rock.

But everyone who listens to these words of mine and does not act on them will be like a stupid man who built his house on sand.

Rain came down, floods rose, gales blew and struck that house, and it fell; and what a fall it had!"

"I am willing. Be cleansed." And his skin-disease was cleansed at once "Mind you tell no one, but go and show yourself to the priest and make the offering prescribed by Moses, as evidence to them." "I will come myself and cure him."

"In truth I tell you, in no one in Israel have I found faith as great as this.

And I tell you that many will come from east and west and sit down with Abraham and Isaac and Jacob at the feast in the kingdom of Heaven;

But the children of the kingdom will be thrown out into the darkness outside, where there will be weeping and grinding of teeth."

And to the centurion Jesus said, "Go back, then; let this be done for you, as your faith demands." And the servant was cured at that moment.

"Foxes have holes and the birds of the air have nests, but the Son of man has nowhere to lay his head."

"Follow me, and leave the dead to bury their dead."

8

"Why are you so frightened, you who have so little faith?"
"Go then,"

"Take comfort, my child, your sins are forgiven."

"Why do you have such wicked thoughts in your hearts?

Now, which of these is easier: to say, `Your sins are forgiven,' or to say, `Get up and walk'?

But to prove to you that the Son of man has authority on earth to forgive sins," then he said to the paralytic, "get up, pick up your bed and go off home."

And the man got up and went home
"Follow me."

"It is not the healthy who need the doctor, but the sick.

Go and learn the meaning of the words: Mercy is what pleases me, not sacrifice. And indeed I came to call not the upright, but sinners."

"Surely the bridegroom's attendants cannot mourn as long as the bridegroom is still with them? But the time will come when the bridegroom is taken away from them, and then they will fast.

No one puts a piece of unshrunken cloth onto an old cloak, because the patch pulls away from the cloak and the tear gets worse.

Nor do people put new wine into old wineskins; otherwise, the skins burst, the wine runs out, and the skins are lost. No; they put new wine in fresh skins and both are preserved."

"Courage, my daughter, your faith has saved you."

`Get out of here; the little girl is not dead; she is asleep."
And when Jesus reached the house the blind men came up to him and he said to them, "Do you believe I can do this?" They said, "Lord, we do."

Then he touched their eyes saying, "According to your faith, let it be done to you."

And their sight returned. Then Jesus sternly warned them, "Take care that no one learns about this."

"The harvest is rich but the laborers are few,

So ask the Lord of the harvest to send out laborers to his harvest."

"Do not make your way to gentile territory, and do not enter any Samaritan town;

Go instead to the lost sheep of the House of Israel.

9

And as you go, proclaim that the kingdom of Heaven is close at hand.

Cure the sick, raise the dead, cleanse those suffering from virulent skin-diseases, drive out devils. You received without charge, give without charge.

Provide yourselves with no gold or silver, not even with coppers for your purses,

With no haversack for the journey or spare tunic or footwear or a staff, for the laborer deserves his keep.

`Whatever town or village you go into, seek out someone worthy and stay with him until you leave.

As you enter his house, salute it,

And if the house deserves it, may your peace come upon it; if it does not, may your peace come back to you.

And if anyone does not welcome you or listen to what you have to say, as you walk out of the house or town shake the dust from your feet.

In truth I tell you, on the Day of Judgement it will be more bearable for Sodom and Gomorrah than for that town.

Look, I am sending you out like sheep among wolves; so be cunning as snakes and yet innocent as doves.

`Be prepared for people to hand you over to sanhedrins and scourge you in their synagogues.

You will be brought before governors and kings for my sake, as evidence to them and to the gentiles.

But when you are handed over, do not worry about how to speak or what to say; what you are to say will be given to you when the time comes,

Because it is not you who will be speaking; the Spirit of your Father will be speaking in you.

`Brother will betray brother to death, and a father his child; children will come forward against their parents and have them put to death.

You will be universally hated on account of my name; but anyone who stands firm to the end will be saved.

If they persecute you in one town, take refuge in the next; and if they persecute you in that, take refuge in another. In truth I tell you, you will not have gone the round of the towns of Israel before the Son of man comes.

`Disciple is not superior to teacher, nor slave to master.

It is enough for disciple to grow to be like teacher, and slave like master. If they have called the master of the house `Beelzebub', how much more the members of his household?

`So do not be afraid of them. Everything now covered up will be uncovered, and everything now hidden will be made clear.

What I say to you in the dark, tell in the daylight; what you hear in whispers, proclaim from the housetops.

`Do not be afraid of those who kill the body but cannot kill the soul; fear him rather who can destroy both body and soul in hell.

Can you not buy two sparrows for a penny? And yet not one falls to the ground without your Father knowing.

Why, every hair on your head has been counted.

So there is no need to be afraid; you are worth more than many sparrows.

`So if anyone declares himself for me in the presence of human beings, I will declare myself for him in the presence of my Father in heaven.

But the one who disowns me in the presence of human beings, I will disown in the presence of my Father in heaven.

`Do not suppose that I have come to bring peace to the earth: it is not peace I have come to bring, but a sword.

For I have come to set son against father, daughter against mother, daughter-in-law against mother-in-law;

A person's enemies will be the members of his own household.

`No one who prefers father or mother to me is worthy of me. No one who prefers son or daughter to me is worthy of me.

Anyone who does not take his cross and follow in my footsteps is not worthy of me.

Anyone who finds his life will lose it; anyone who loses his life for my sake will find it.

`Anyone who welcomes you welcomes me; and anyone who welcomes me welcomes the one who sent me.

`Anyone who welcomes a prophet because he is a prophet will have a prophet's reward; and anyone who welcomes an upright person because he is upright will have the reward of an upright person.

`If anyone gives so much as a cup of cold water to one of these little ones because he is a disciple, then in truth I tell you, he will most certainly not go without his reward."

Love 3

JOHN THE BAPTIST

Jesus answered, "Go back and tell John what you hear and see;

The blind see again, and the lame walk, those suffering from virulent skin-diseases are cleansed, and the deaf hear, the dead are raised to life and the good news is proclaimed to the poor;

And blessed is anyone who does not find me a cause of falling."

As the men were leaving, Jesus began to talk to the people about John, "What did you go out into the desert to see? A reed swaying in the breeze? No?

Then what did you go out to see? A man wearing fine clothes? Look, those who wear fine clothes are to be found in palaces.

Then what did you go out for? To see a prophet? Yes, I tell you, and much more than a prophet:

He is the one of whom scripture says: Look, I am going to send my messenger in front of you to prepare your way before you.

`In truth I tell you, of all the children born to women, there has never been anyone greater than John the Baptist; yet the least in the kingdom of Heaven is greater than he.

Since John the Baptist came, up to this present time, the kingdom of Heaven has been subjected to violence and the violent are taking it by storm.

Because it was towards John that all the prophecies of the prophets and of the Law were leading;

And he, if you will believe me, is the Elijah who was to return.

Anyone who has ears should listen!

JESUS CONDEMNS HIS CONTEMPORARIES

`What comparison can I find for this generation? It is like children shouting to each other as they sit in the market place:

We played the pipes for you,
and you wouldn't dance;
we sang dirges,
and you wouldn't be mourners.

`For John came, neither eating nor drinking, and they say, `He is possessed.'

The Son of man came, eating and drinking, and they say, `Look, a glutton and a drunkard, a friend of tax collectors and sinners.' Yet wisdom is justified by her deeds."

`Alas for you, Chorazin! Alas for you, Bethsaida! For if the miracles done in you had been done in Tyre and Sidon, they would have repented long ago in sackcloth and ashes.

Still, I tell you that it will be more bearable for Tyre and Sidon on Judgement Day than for you.

And as for you, Capernaum, did you want to be raised as high as heaven? You shall be flung down to hell. For if the miracles done in you had been done in Sodom, it would have been standing yet.

Still, I tell you that it will be more bearable for Sodom on Judgement Day than for you."

At that time Jesus exclaimed, "I bless you, Father, Lord of heaven and of earth, for hiding these things from the learned and the clever and revealing them to little children.

Yes, Father, for that is what it pleased you to do.

Everything has been entrusted to me by my Father; and no one knows the Son except the Father, just as no one knows the Father except the Son and those to whom the Son chooses to reveal him.

`Come to me, all you who labor and are overburdened, and I will give you rest.

Shoulder my yoke and learn from me, for I am gentle and humble in heart, and you will find rest for your souls.

Yes, my yoke is easy and my burden light."

But he said to them, "Have you not read what David did when he and his followers were hungry,

How he went into the house of God and they ate the loaves of the offering although neither he nor his followers were permitted to eat them, but only the priests?

Or again, have you not read in the Law that on the Sabbath day the Temple priests break the Sabbath without committing any fault?

Now here, I tell you, is something greater than the Temple.

And if you had understood the meaning of the words: Mercy is what pleases me, not sacrifice, you would not have condemned the blameless.

For the Son of man is master of the Sabbath."

But he said to them, "If any one of you here had only one sheep and it fell down a hole on the Sabbath day, would he not get hold of it and lift it out?

Now a man is far more important than a sheep, so it follows that it is permitted on the Sabbath day to do good."

Then he said to the man, "Stretch out your hand." He stretched it out and his hand was restored, as sound as the other one.

Knowing what was in their minds he said to them, "Every kingdom divided against itself is heading for ruin; and no town, no household divided against itself can last.

Now if Satan drives out Satan, he is divided against himself; so how can his kingdom last?

And if it is through Beelzebub that I drive devils out, through whom do your own experts drive them out? They shall be your judges, then.

But if it is through the Spirit of God that I drive out devils, then be sure that the kingdom of God has caught you unawares.

`Or again, how can anyone make his way into a strong man's house and plunder his property unless he has first tied up the strong man? Only then can he plunder his house.

`Anyone who is not with me is against me, and anyone who does not gather in with me throws away.

And so I tell you, every human sin and blasphemy will be forgiven, but blasphemy against the Spirit will not be forgiven.

And anyone who says a word against the Son of man will be forgiven; but no one who speaks against the Holy Spirit will be forgiven either in this world or in the next.

He replied, "It is an evil and unfaithful generation that asks for a sign! The only sign it will be given is the sign of the prophet Jonah.

For as Jonah remained in the belly of the sea-monster for three days and three nights, so will the Son of man be in the heart of the earth for three days and three nights.

On Judgement Day the men of Nineveh will appear against this generation and they will be its condemnation, because when Jonah preached they repented; and look, there is something greater than Jonah here.

On Judgement Day the Queen of the South will appear against this generation and be its condemnation, because she came from the ends of the earth to hear the wisdom of Solomon; and look, there is something greater than Solomon here.

THE RETURN OF THE UNCLEAN SPIRIT

`When an unclean spirit goes out of someone it wanders through waterless country looking for a place to rest, and cannot find one.

Then it says, `I will return to the home I came from.' But on arrival, finding it unoccupied, swept and tidied,

It then goes off and collects seven other spirits more wicked than itself, and they go in and set up house there, and so that person ends up worse off than before. That is what will happen to this wicked generation."

But to the man who told him this Jesus replied, "Who is my mother? Who are my brothers?"

And stretching out his hand towards his disciples he said, "Here are my mother and my brothers.

Anyone who does the will of my Father in heaven is my brother and sister and mother."

Love 4

WHY JESUS SPEAKS IN PARABLES

He said, "Listen, a sower went out to sow.

As he sowed, some seeds fell on the edge of the path, and the birds came and ate them up.

Others fell on patches of rock where they found little soil and sprang up at once, because there was no depth of earth;

But as soon as the sun came up they were scorched and, not having any roots, they withered away.

Others fell among thorns, and the thorns grew up and choked them.

Others fell on rich soil and produced their crop, some a hundredfold, some sixty, some thirty.

Anyone who has ears should listen!"

Then the disciples went up to him and asked, "Why do you talk to them in parables?"

In answer, he said, "Because to you is granted to understand the mysteries of the kingdom of Heaven, but to them it is not granted.

Anyone who has will be given more and will have more than enough; but anyone who has not will be deprived even of what he has.

The reason I talk to them in parables is that they look without seeing and listen without hearing or understanding.

So in their case what was spoken by the prophet Isaiah is being fulfilled:
Listen and listen, but never understand!
Look and look, but never perceive!

This people's heart has grown coarse,
their ears dulled, they have shut their eyes tight
to avoid using their eyes to see, their ears to hear,
their heart to understand,
changing their ways and being healed by me.

`But blessed are your eyes because they see, your ears because they hear!

In truth I tell you, many prophets and upright people longed to see what you see, and never saw it; to hear what you hear, and never heard it.

THE PARABLE OF THE SOWER EXPLAINED

`So pay attention to the parable of the sower.

When anyone hears the word of the kingdom without understanding, the Evil One comes and carries off what was sown in his heart: this is the seed sown on the edge of the path.

The seed sown on patches of rock is someone who hears the word and welcomes it at once with joy.

But such a person has no root deep down and does not last; should some trial come, or some persecution on account of the word, at once he falls away.

The seed sown in thorns is someone who hears the word, but the worry of the world and the lure of riches choke the word and so it produces nothing.

And the seed sown in rich soil is someone who hears the word and understands it; this is the one who yields a harvest and produces now a hundredfold, now sixty, now thirty."

PARABLE OF THE DARNEL

He put another parable before them, "The kingdom of Heaven may be compared to a man who sowed good seed in his field.

While everybody was asleep his enemy came, sowed darnel all among the wheat, and made off.

When the new wheat sprouted and ripened, then the darnel appeared as well.

The owner's laborers went to him and said, `Sir, was it not good seed that you sowed in your field? If so, where does the darnel come from?'

He said to them, `Some enemy has done this.' And the laborers said, `Do you want us to go and weed it out?'

But he said, `No, because when you weed out the darnel you might pull up the wheat with it.

Let them both grow till the harvest; and at harvest time I shall say to the reapers: First collect the darnel and tie it in bundles to be burnt, then gather the wheat into my barn.' "

PARABLE OF THE MUSTARD SEED

He put another parable before them, "The kingdom of Heaven is like a mustard seed which a man took and sowed in his field.

It is the smallest of all the seeds, but when it has grown it is the biggest of shrubs and becomes a tree, so that the birds of the air can come and shelter in its branches."

17

PARABLE OF THE YEAST

He told them another parable, "The kingdom of Heaven is like the yeast a woman took and mixed in with three measures of flour till it was leavened all through."

Then, leaving the crowds, he went to the house; and his disciples came to him and said, "Explain to us the parable about the darnel in the field."

He said in reply, "The sower of the good seed is the Son of man.

The field is the world; the good seed is the subjects of the kingdom; the darnel, the subjects of the Evil One;

The enemy who sowed it, the devil; the harvest is the end of the world; the reapers are the angels.

Well then, just as the darnel is gathered up and burnt in the fire, so it will be at the end of time.

The Son of man will send his angels and they will gather out of his kingdom all causes of falling and all who do evil,

And throw them into the blazing furnace, where there will be weeping and grinding of teeth.

Then the upright will shine like the sun in the kingdom of their Father. Anyone who has ears should listen!

PARABLES OF THE TREASURE AND OF THE PEARL

'The kingdom of Heaven is like treasure hidden in a field which someone has found; he hides it again, goes off in his joy, sells everything he owns and buys the field.

`Again, the kingdom of Heaven is like a merchant looking for fine pearls;

When he finds one of great value he goes and sells everything he owns and buys it.

PARABLE OF THE DRAGNET

`Again, the kingdom of Heaven is like a dragnet that is cast in the sea and brings in a haul of all kinds of fish.

When it is full, the fishermen bring it ashore; then, sitting down, they collect the good ones in baskets and throw away those that are no use.

This is how it will be at the end of time: the angels will appear and separate the wicked from the upright, to throw them into the blazing furnace, where there will be weeping and grinding of teeth.

CONCLUSION

`Have you understood all these?" They said, "Yes."

And he said to them, "Well then, every scribe who becomes a disciple of the kingdom of Heaven is like a householder who brings out from his storeroom new things as well as old."

And they would not accept him. But Jesus said to them, "A prophet is despised only in his own country and in his own house,"

LOAVES

FIRST MIRACLE OF THE LOAVES

Jesus replied, "There is no need for them to go: give them something to eat yourselves."

But they answered, "All we have with us is five loaves and two fish."

So he said, "Bring them here to me."

But at once Jesus called out to them, saying, "Courage! It's me! Don't be afraid."

It was Peter who answered. "Lord," he said, "if it is you, tell me to come to you across the water."

Jesus said, "Come." Then Peter got out of the boat and started walking towards Jesus across the water,

But then noticing the wind, he took fright and began to sink. "Lord," he cried, "save me!"

Jesus put out his hand at once and held him. "You have so little faith," he said, "why did you doubt?"

And as they got into the boat the wind dropped.

The men in the boat bowed down before him and said, "Truly, you are the Son of God."

He answered, "And why do you break away from the commandment of God for the sake of your tradition?

For God said, `Honor your father and your mother' and `Anyone who curses his father or mother will be put to death.'

But you say, `If anyone says to his father or mother: Anything I might have used to help you is dedicated to God,

He is rid of his duty to father or mother.' In this way you have made God's word ineffective by means of your tradition.

Hypocrites! How rightly Isaiah prophesied about you when he said:

This people honors me only with lip-service, while their hearts are far from me.

Their reverence of me is worthless; the lessons they teach are nothing but human commandments."

He called the people to him and said, "Listen, and understand.

What goes into the mouth does not make anyone unclean; it is what comes out of the mouth that makes someone unclean."

Then the disciples came to him and said, "Do you know that the Pharisees were shocked when they heard what you said?"

He replied, "Any plant my heavenly Father has not planted will be pulled up by the roots.

Leave them alone. They are blind leaders of the blind; and if one blind person leads another, both will fall into a pit."

Jesus replied, "Even you, don't you yet understand?

Can't you see that whatever goes into the mouth passes through the stomach and is discharged into the sewer?

But whatever comes out of the mouth comes from the heart, and it is this that makes someone unclean. For from the heart come evil intentions: murder, adultery, fornication, theft, perjury, slander. These are the things that make a person unclean. But eating with unwashed hands does not make anyone unclean."

He said in reply, "I was sent only to the lost sheep of the House of Israel."

But the woman had come up and was bowing low before him. "Lord," she said, "help me."

He replied, "It is not fair to take the children's food and throw it to little dogs."

She retorted, "Ah yes, Lord; but even little dogs eat the scraps that fall from their masters' table."

Then Jesus answered her, "Woman, you have great faith. Let your desire be granted." And from that moment her daughter was well again.

SECOND MIRACLE OF THE LOAVES

But Jesus called his disciples to him and said, "I feel sorry for all these people; they have been with me for three days now and have nothing to eat. I do not want to send them off hungry, or they might collapse on the way."

The disciples said to him, "Where in a deserted place could we get sufficient bread for such a large crowd to have enough to eat?"

Jesus said to them, "How many loaves have you?" They said, "Seven, and a few small fish."

He replied, "In the evening you say, `It will be fine; there's a red sky,'

And in the morning, `Stormy weather today; the sky is red and overcast.' You know how to read the face of the sky, but you cannot read the signs of the times.

It is an evil and unfaithful generation asking for a sign, and the only sign it will be given is the sign of Jonah." And he left them and went off.

Jesus said to them, "Keep your eyes open, and be on your guard against the yeast of the Pharisees and Sadducees."

And they said among themselves, "It is because we have not brought any bread."

Jesus knew it, and he said, "You have so little faith, why are you talking among yourselves about having no bread?

Do you still not understand? Do you not remember the five loaves for the five thousand and the number of baskets you collected?

Or the seven loaves for the four thousand and the number of baskets you collected?

How could you fail to understand that I was not talking about bread? What I said was: Beware of the yeast of the Pharisees and Sadducees."

When Jesus came to the region of Caesarea Philippi he put this question to his disciples, "Who do people say the Son of man is?"

And they said, "Some say John the Baptist, some Elijah, and others Jeremiah or one of the prophets."

`But you," he said, "who do you say I am?"

Then Simon Peter spoke up and said, "You are the Christ, the Son of the living God."

Jesus replied, "Simon son of Jonah, you are a blessed man! Because it was no human agency that revealed this to you but my Father in heaven.

So I now say to you: You are Peter and on this rock I will build my community. And the gates of the underworld can never overpower it.

I will give you the keys of the kingdom of Heaven: whatever you bind on earth will be bound in heaven; whatever you loose on earth will be loosed in heaven."

Then, taking him aside, Peter started to rebuke him. "Heaven preserve you, Lord," he said, "this must not happen to you."

But he turned and said to Peter, "Get behind me, Satan! You are an obstacle in my path, because you are thinking not as God thinks but as human beings do."

22

LOVE 6

THE CONDITION OF FOLLOWING CHRIST

Then Jesus said to his disciples, "If anyone wants to be a follower of mine, let him renounce himself and take up his cross and follow me.

Anyone who wants to save his life will lose it; but anyone who loses his life for my sake will find it.

What, then, will anyone gain by winning the whole world and forfeiting his life? Or what can anyone offer in exchange for his life?

'For the Son of man is going to come in the glory of his Father with his angels, and then he will reward each one according to his behavior.

In truth I tell you, there are some standing here who will not taste death before they see the Son of man coming with his kingdom."

Then Peter spoke to Jesus. "Lord," he said, "it is wonderful for us to be here; if you want me to, I will make three shelters here, one for you, one for Moses and one for Elijah."

He was still speaking when suddenly a bright cloud covered them with shadow, and suddenly from the cloud there came a voice which said, "This is my Son, the Beloved; he enjoys my favor. Listen to him."

When they heard this, the disciples fell on their faces, overcome with fear.

But Jesus came up and touched them, saying, "Stand up, do not be afraid."

As they came down from the mountain Jesus gave them this order, "Tell no one about this vision until the Son of man has risen from the dead."

And the disciples put this question to him, "Why then do the scribes say that Elijah must come first?"

He replied, "Elijah is indeed coming, and he will set everything right again;

However, I tell you that Elijah has come already and they did not recognize him but treated him as they pleased; and the Son of man will suffer similarly at their hands."

In reply, Jesus said, "Faithless and perverse generation! How much longer must I be with you? How much longer must I put up with you? Bring him here to me."

And when Jesus rebuked it the devil came out of the boy, who was cured from that moment.

Then the disciples came privately to Jesus. "Why were we unable to drive it out?" they asked.

He answered, "Because you have so little faith. In truth I tell you, if your faith is the size of a mustard seed you will say to this mountain, `Move from here to there,' and it will move; nothing will be impossible for you."

When they were together in Galilee, Jesus said to them, "The Son of man is going to be delivered into the power of men;

They will put him to death, and on the third day he will be raised up again."

`Yes," he replied, and went into the house. But before he could speak, Jesus said, "Simon, what is your opinion? From whom do earthly kings take toll or tribute? From their sons or from foreigners?"

And when he replied, "From foreigners," Jesus said, "Well then, the sons are exempt.

However, so that we shall not be the downfall of others, go to the lake and cast a hook; take the first fish that rises, open its mouth and there you will find a shekel; take it and give it to them for me and for yourself."

Then he said, "In truth I tell you, unless you change and become like little children you will never enter the kingdom of Heaven.

And so, the one who makes himself as little as this little child is the greatest in the kingdom of Heaven.

ON LEADING OTHERS ASTRAY

`Anyone who welcomes one little child like this in my name welcomes me.

But anyone who is the downfall of one of these little ones who have faith in me would be better drowned in the depths of the sea with a great millstone round his neck.

Alas for the world that there should be such causes of falling! Causes of falling indeed there must be, but alas for anyone who provides them!

`If your hand or your foot should be your downfall, cut it off and throw it away: it is better for you to enter into life crippled or lame, than to have two hands or two feet and be thrown into eternal fire.

And if your eye should be your downfall, tear it out and throw it away: it is better for you to enter into life with one eye, than to have two eyes and be thrown into the hell of fire.

`See that you never despise any of these little ones, for I tell you that their angels in heaven are continually in the presence of my Father in heaven.

THE LOST SHEEP

`Tell me. Suppose a man has a hundred sheep and one of them strays; will he not leave the ninety-nine on the hillside and go in search of the stray?

In truth I tell you, if he finds it, it gives him more joy than do the ninety-nine that did not stray at all.

Similarly, it is never the will of your Father in heaven that one of these little ones should be lost.

BROTHERLY CORRECTION

`If your brother does something wrong, go and have it out with him alone, between your two selves. If he listens to you, you have won back your brother.

If he does not listen, take one or two others along with you: whatever the misdemeanor, the evidence of two or three witnesses is required to sustain the charge.

But if he refuses to listen to these, report it to the community; and if he refuses to listen to the community, treat him like a gentile or a tax collector.

`In truth I tell you, whatever you bind on earth will be bound in heaven; whatever you loose on earth will be loosed in heaven.

PRAYER IN COMMON

`In truth I tell you once again, if two of you on earth agree to ask anything at all, it will be granted to you by my Father in heaven.

For where two or three meet in my name, I am there among them."

FORGIVENESS OF INJURIES

Then Peter went up to him and said, "Lord, how often must I forgive my brother if he wrongs me? As often as seven times?"

Jesus answered, "Not seven, I tell you, but seventy-seven times.

PARABLE OF THE UNFORGIVING DEBTOR

`And so the kingdom of Heaven may be compared to a king who decided to settle his accounts with his servants.

When the reckoning began, they brought him a man who owed ten thousand talents;

He had no means of paying, so his master gave orders that he should be sold, together with his wife and children and all his possessions, to meet the debt.

At this, the servant threw himself down at his master's feet, with the words, `Be patient with me and I will pay the whole sum.'

And the servant's master felt so sorry for him that he let him go and cancelled the debt.

Now as this servant went out, he happened to meet a fellow-servant who owed him one hundred denarii; and he seized him by the throat and began to throttle him, saying, `Pay what you owe me.'

His fellow servant fell at his feet and appealed to him, saying, `Be patient with me and I will pay you.'

But the other would not agree; on the contrary, he had him thrown into prison till he should pay the debt.

His fellow servants were deeply distressed when they saw what had happened, and they went to their master and reported the whole affair to him.

Then the master sent for the man and said to him, `You wicked servant; I cancelled all that debt of yours when you appealed to me.

Were you not bound, then, to have pity on your fellow-servant just as I had pity on you?'

And in his anger the master handed him over to the torturers till he should pay all his debt.

And that is how my heavenly Father will deal with you unless you each forgive your brother from your heart."

He answered, "Have you not read that the Creator from the beginning made them male and female

And that he said: This is why a man leaves his father and mother and becomes attached to his wife, and the two become one flesh?

They are no longer two, therefore, but one flesh. So then, what God has united, human beings must not divide."

They said to him, "Then why did Moses command that a writ of dismissal should be given in cases of divorce?"

He said to them, "It was because you were so hard-hearted, that Moses allowed you to divorce your wives, but it was not like this from the beginning.

Now I say this to you: anyone who divorces his wife, I am not speaking of an illicit marriage, and marries another, is guilty of adultery."

But he replied, "It is not everyone who can accept what I have said, but only those to whom it is granted.

There are eunuchs born so from their mother's womb, there are eunuchs made so by human agency and there are eunuchs who have made themselves so for the sake of the kingdom of Heaven. Let anyone accept this who can."

But Jesus said, "Let the little children alone, and do not stop them from coming to me; for it is to such as these that the kingdom of Heaven belongs."

Jesus said to him, "Why do you ask me about what is good? There is one alone who is good. But if you wish to enter into life, keep the commandments."

NEW TESTAMENT COMMANDMENTS

He said, "Which ones?" Jesus replied, "These:

You shall not kill.
You shall not commit adultery.
You shall not steal.
You shall not give false witness.
Honor your father and your mother.
You shall love your neighbor as yourself."

Jesus said, "If you wish to be perfect, go and sell your possessions and give the money to the poor, and you will have treasure in heaven; then come, follow me."

Then Jesus said to his disciples, "In truth I tell you, it is hard for someone rich to enter the kingdom of Heaven.
Yes, I tell you again, it is easier for a camel to pass through the eye of a needle than for someone rich to enter the kingdom of Heaven."

Jesus gazed at them. "By human resources", he told them, "this is impossible; for God everything is possible."

Jesus said to them, "In truth I tell you, when everything is made new again and the Son of man is seated on his throne of glory, you yourselves will sit on twelve thrones to judge the twelve tribes of Israel.

And everyone who has left houses, brothers, sisters, father, mother, children or land for the sake of my name will receive a hundred times as much, and also inherit eternal life.

`Many who are first will be last, and the last, first."

`Now the kingdom of Heaven is like a landowner going out at daybreak to hire workers for his vineyard.

He made an agreement with the workers for one denarius a day and sent them to his vineyard.

Going out at about the third hour he saw others standing idle in the market place

And said to them, `You go to my vineyard too and I will give you a fair wage.'

So they went. At about the sixth hour and again at about the ninth hour, he went out and did the same.

Then at about the eleventh hour he went out and found more men standing around, and he said to them, `Why have you been standing here idle all day?'

`Because no one has hired us,' they answered. He said to them, "`You go into my vineyard too.'

In the evening, the owner of the vineyard said to his bailiff, `Call the workers and pay them their wages, starting with the last arrivals and ending with the first.'

So those who were hired at about the eleventh hour came forward and received one denarius each.

When the first came, they expected to get more, but they too received one denarius each.

They took it, but grumbled at the landowner saying,

`The men who came last have done only one hour, and you have treated them the same as us, though we have done a heavy day's work in all the heat.'

He answered one of them and said, `My friend, I am not being unjust to you; did we not agree on one denarius?
Take your earnings and go. I choose to pay the last comer as much as I pay you.

Have I no right to do what I like with my own? Why should you be envious because I am generous?'

Thus the last will be first, and the first, last."

LOVE 8

THIRD PROPHECY OF THE PASSION

Jesus was going up to Jerusalem, and on the road he took the Twelve aside by themselves and said to them,

'Look, we are going up to Jerusalem, and the Son of man is about to be handed over to the chief priests and scribes. They will condemn him to death

And will hand him over to the gentiles to be mocked and scourged and crucified; and on the third day he will be raised up again."

And he said to her, "What is it you want?" She said to him, "Promise that these two sons of mine may sit one at your right hand and the other at your left in your kingdom."

Jesus answered, "You do not know what you are asking. Can you drink the cup that I am going to drink?" They replied, "We can."

He said to them, "Very well; you shall drink my cup, but as for seats at my right hand and my left, these are not mine to grant; they belong to those to whom they have been allotted by my Father."

But Jesus called them to him and said, "You know that among the gentiles the rulers lord it over them, and great men make their authority felt.

Among you this is not to happen. No; anyone who wants to become great among you must be your servant,

And anyone who wants to be first among you must be your slave,

Just as the Son of man came not to be served but to serve, and to give his life as a ransom for many."

And now there were two blind men sitting at the side of the road. When they heard that it was Jesus who was passing by, they shouted, "Lord! Have pity on us, son of David."

And the crowd scolded them and told them to keep quiet, but they only shouted the louder, "Lord! Have pity on us, son of David."

Jesus stopped, called them over and said, "What do you want me to do for you?"

They said to him, "Lord, let us have our sight back."

Jesus felt pity for them and touched their eyes, and at once their sight returned and they followed him.

Saying to them, "Go to the village facing you, and you will at once find a tethered donkey and a colt with her. Untie them and bring them to me.

If anyone says anything to you, you are to say, `The Master needs him or her and will send him or her back at once.' "

Say to the daughter of Zion:
Look, your king is approaching,
humble and riding on a donkey
and on a colt, the foal of a beast of burden.

He said to them, "According to scripture, my house will be called a house of prayer; but you are turning it into a bandits' den."

`Do you hear what they are saying?" Jesus answered, "Yes. Have you never read this?
By the mouths of children, babes in arms,
you have made sure of praise?"

Seeing a fig tree by the road, he went up to it and found nothing on it but leaves. And he said to it, "May you never bear fruit again," and instantly the fig tree withered.

The disciples were amazed when they saw it and said, "How is it that the fig tree withered instantly?"

Jesus answered, "In truth I tell you, if you have faith and do not doubt at all, not only will you do what I have done to the fig tree, but even if you say to this mountain, `Be pulled up and thrown into the sea,' it will be done.

And if you have faith, everything you ask for in prayer, you will receive."

In reply Jesus said to them, "And I will ask you a question, just one; if you tell me the answer to it, then I will tell you my authority for acting like this.

John's baptism: what was its origin, heavenly or human?" And they argued this way among themselves, "If we say heavenly, he will retort to us, `Then why did you refuse to believe him?';

But if we say human, we have the people to fear, for they all hold that John was a prophet."

So their reply to Jesus was, "We do not know." And he retorted to them, "Nor will I tell you my authority for acting like this."

`What is your opinion? A man had two sons. He went and said to the first, `My boy, go and work in the vineyard today.'

He answered, `I will not go,' but afterwards thought better of it and went.

The man then went and said the same thing to the second who answered, `Certainly, sir,' but did not go.

Which of the two did the father's will?" They said, "The first." Jesus said to them, "In truth I tell you, tax collectors and prostitutes are making their way into the kingdom of God before you.

For John came to you, showing the way of uprightness, but you did not believe him, and yet the tax collectors and prostitutes did. Even after seeing that, you refused to think better of it and believe in him.

`Listen to another parable. There was a man, a landowner, who planted a vineyard; he fenced it round, dug a winepress in it and built a tower; then he leased it to tenants and went abroad.

When vintage time drew near he sent his servants to the tenants to collect his produce.

But the tenants seized his servants, thrashed one, killed another and stoned a third.

Next he sent some more servants, this time a larger number, and they dealt with them in the same way.

Finally he sent his son to them thinking, `They will respect my son.'

But when the tenants saw the son, they said to each other, `This is the heir. Come on, let us kill him and take over his inheritance.'

So they seized him and threw him out of the vineyard and killed him.

Now when the owner of the vineyard comes, what will he do to those tenants?"

They answered, "He will bring those wretches to a wretched end and lease the vineyard to other tenants who will deliver the produce to him at the proper time."

Jesus said to them, "Have you never read in the scriptures:
The stone which the builders rejected
has become the cornerstone;
this is the Lord's doing
and we marvel at it?

`I tell you, then, that the kingdom of God will be taken from you and given to a people who will produce its fruit."

SECOND GROUP OF PARABLES

Jesus began to speak to them in parables once again,

`The kingdom of Heaven may be compared to a king who gave a feast for his son's wedding.

He sent his servants to call those who had been invited, but they would not come.

Next he sent some more servants with the words, `Tell those who have been invited: Look, my banquet is all prepared, my oxen and fattened cattle have been slaughtered, and everything is ready. Come to the wedding.'

But they were not interested: one went off to his farm, another to his business,

And the rest seized his servants, maltreated them and killed them.

The king was furious. He dispatched his troops, destroyed those murderers and burnt their town.

Then he said to his servants, `The wedding is ready; but as those who were invited proved to be unworthy,

Go to the main crossroads and invite everyone you can find to come to the wedding.'

So these servants went out onto the roads and collected together everyone they could find, bad and good alike; and the wedding hall was filled with guests.

When the king came in to look at the guests he noticed one man who was not wearing a wedding garment,

And said to him, `How did you get in here, my friend, without a wedding garment?' And the man was silent.

Then the king said to the attendants, `Bind him hand and foot and throw him into the darkness outside, where there will be weeping and grinding of teeth.'

For many are invited but not all are chosen."

And he said, "Whose portrait is this? Whose title?"

Show me the money you pay the tax with." They handed him a denarius,

But Jesus was aware of their malice and replied, "You hypocrites! Why are you putting me to the test?

They replied, "Caesar's." "Then he said to them, "Very well, pay Caesar what belongs to Caesar, and God what belongs to God."

Jesus answered them, "You are wrong, because you understand neither the scriptures nor the power of God.

For at the resurrection men and women do not marry; no, they are like the angels in heaven.

And as for the resurrection of the dead, have you never read what God himself said to you: I am the God of Abraham, the God of Isaac and the God of Jacob? He is God, not of the dead, but of the living."

`Master, which is the greatest commandment of the Law?"

THE 2 MOST IMPORTANT COMMANDMENTS ACCORDING TO CHRIST

Jesus said to him, "You must love the Lord your God with all your heart, with all your soul, and with all your mind.

This is the greatest and the first commandment.

The second resembles it: You must love your neighbor as yourself.

On these two commandments hang the whole Law, and the Prophets too."

While the Pharisees were gathered round, Jesus put to them this question,

`What is your opinion about the Christ? Whose son is he?" They told him, "David's."

He said to them, "Then how is it that David, moved by the Spirit, calls him Lord, where he says:

The Lord declared to my Lord,
take your seat at my right hand,
till I have made your enemies
your footstool?

`If David calls him Lord, how then can he be his son?"

`The scribes and the Pharisees occupy the chair of Moses.

You must therefore do and observe what they tell you; but do not be guided by what they do, since they do not practice what they preach.

They tie up heavy burdens and lay them on people's shoulders, but will they lift a finger to move them? Not they!

Everything they do is done to attract attention, like wearing broader headbands and longer tassels,

Like wanting to take the place of honor at banquets and the front seats in the synagogues,

Being greeted respectfully in the market squares and having people call them Rabbi.

`You, however, must not allow yourselves to be called Rabbi, since you have only one Master, and you are all brothers.

You must call no one on earth your father, since you have only one Father, and he is in heaven.

Nor must you allow yourselves to be called teachers, for you have only one Teacher, the Christ.

The greatest among you must be your servant.

Anyone who raises himself up will be humbled, and anyone who humbles himself will be raised up.

THE SEVENFOLD INDICTMENT OF THE SCRIBES AND PHARISEES

`Alas for you, scribes and Pharisees, you hypocrites! You shut up the kingdom of Heaven in people's faces, neither going in yourselves nor allowing others to go in who want to.

`Alas for you, scribes and Pharisees, you hypocrites! You travel over sea and land to make a single proselyte, and anyone who becomes one you make twice as fit for hell as you are.

`Alas for you, blind guides! You say, `If anyone swears by the Temple, it has no force; but anyone who swears by the gold of the Temple is bound.'

Fools and blind! For which is of greater value, the gold or the Temple that makes the gold sacred?

Again, `If anyone swears by the altar it has no force; but anyone who swears by the offering on the altar, is bound.'

You blind men! For which is of greater worth, the offering or the altar that makes the offering sacred?

Therefore, someone who swears by the altar is swearing by that and by everything on it.

And someone who swears by the Temple is swearing by that and by the One who dwells in it.

And someone who swears by heaven is swearing by the throne of God and by the One who is seated there.

`Alas for you, scribes and Pharisees, you hypocrites! You pay your tithe of mint and dill and cumin and have neglected the weightier matters of the Law, justice, mercy, and good faith! These you should have practiced, those not neglected.

You blind guides, straining out gnats and swallowing camels!

`Alas for you, scribes and Pharisees, you hypocrites! You clean the outside of cup and dish and leave the inside full of extortion and intemperance.

Blind Pharisee! Clean the inside of cup and dish first so that it and the outside are both clean.

`Alas for you, scribes and Pharisees, you hypocrites! You are like whitewashed tombs that look handsome on the outside, but inside are full of the bones of the dead and every kind of corruption.

In just the same way, from the outside you look upright, but inside you are full of hypocrisy and lawlessness.

`Alas for you, scribes and Pharisees, you hypocrites! You build the sepulchres of the prophets and decorate the tombs of the upright,

Saying, `We would never have joined in shedding the blood of the prophets, had we lived in our ancestors' day.'

So! Your own evidence tells against you! You are the children of those who murdered the prophets!

Very well then, finish off the work that your ancestors began.

THEIR CRIMES AND APPROACHING PUNISHMENT

`You serpents, brood of vipers, how can you escape being condemned to hell?

This is why, look, I am sending you prophets and wise men and scribes; some you will slaughter and crucify, some you will scourge in your synagogues and hunt from town to town;

And so you will draw down on yourselves the blood of every upright person that has been shed on earth, from the blood of Abel the holy to the blood of Zechariah son of Barachiah whom you murdered between the sanctuary and the altar.

In truth I tell you, it will all recoil on this generation.

JERUSALEM ADMONISHED

`Jerusalem, Jerusalem, you that kill the prophets and stone those who are sent to you! How often have I longed to gather your children together, as a hen gathers her chicks under her wings, and you refused!

Look! Your house will be deserted,

For, I promise, you shall not see me any more until you are saying: Blessed is he who is coming in the name of the Lord!"

Jesus left the Temple, and as he was going away his disciples came up to draw his attention to the Temple buildings.

He said to them in reply, "You see all these? In truth I tell you, not a single stone here will be left on another: everything will be pulled down."

And while he was sitting on the Mount of Olives the disciples came and asked him when they were by themselves, "Tell us, when is this going to happen, and what sign will there be of your coming and of the end of the world?"

THE BEGINNING OF SORROWS

And Jesus answered them, "Take care that no one deceives you,

Because many will come using my name and saying, `I am the Christ,' and they will deceive many.

You will hear of wars and rumors of wars; see that you are not alarmed, for this is something that must happen, but the end will not be yet.

For nation will fight against nation, and kingdom against kingdom. There will be famines and earthquakes in various places.

All this is only the beginning of the birth pangs.

`Then you will be handed over to be tortured and put to death; and you will be hated by all nations on account of my name.

And then many will fall away; people will betray one another and hate one another.

Many false prophets will arise; they will deceive many,

And with the increase of lawlessness, love in most people will grow cold;

But anyone who stands firm to the end will be saved.

`This good news of the kingdom will be proclaimed to the whole world as evidence to the nations. And then the end will come.

THE GREAT TRIBULATION OF JERUSALEM

`So when you see the appalling abomination, of which the prophet Daniel spoke, set up in the holy place (let the reader understand),

Then those in Judea must escape to the mountains;

If anyone is on the housetop, he must not come down to collect his belongings from the house;

If anyone is in the fields, he must not turn back to fetch his cloak.

Alas for those with child, or with babies at the breast, when those days come!

Pray that you will not have to make your escape in winter or on a Sabbath.

For then there will be great distress, unparalleled since the world began, and such as will never be again.

And if that time had not been shortened, no human being would have survived; but shortened that time shall be, for the sake of those who are chosen.

`If anyone says to you then, `Look, here is the Christ,' or `Over here,' do not believe it;

For false Christs and false prophets will arise and provide great signs and portents, enough to deceive even the elect, if that were possible.

Look! I have given you warning.

THE COMING OF THE SON OF MAN

`If, then, they say to you, `Look, he is in the desert,' do not go there; `Look, he is in some hiding place,' do not believe it;

Because the coming of the Son of man will be like lightning striking in the east and flashing far into the west.

Wherever the corpse is, that is where the vultures will gather.

THE UNIVERSAL SIGNIFICANCE OF THIS COMING

`Immediately after the distress of those days the sun will be darkened, the moon will not give its light, the stars will fall from the sky and the powers of the heavens will be shaken.

And then the sign of the Son of man will appear in heaven; then, too, all the peoples of the earth will beat their breasts; and they will see the Son of man coming on the clouds of heaven with power and great glory.

And he will send his angels with a loud trumpet to gather his elect from the four winds, from one end of heaven to the other.

THE TIME OF THIS COMING

`Take the fig tree as a parable: as soon as its twigs grow supple and its leaves come out, you know that summer is near.

So with you when you see all these things: know that he is near, right at the gates.

In truth I tell you, before this generation has passed away, all these things will have taken place.

Sky and earth will pass away, but my words will never pass away.

But as for that day and hour, nobody knows it, neither the angels of heaven, nor the Son, no one but the Father alone.

BE ON THE ALERT

`As it was in Noah's day, so will it be when the Son of man comes.

For in those days before the Flood people were eating, drinking, taking wives, taking husbands, right up to the day Noah went into the ark,

And they suspected nothing till the Flood came and swept them all away. This is what it will be like when the Son of man comes.

Then of two men in the fields, one is taken, one left;

Of two women grinding at the mill, one is taken, one left.

`So stay awake, because you do not know the day when your master is coming.

You may be quite sure of this, that if the householder had known at what time of the night the burglar would come, he would have stayed awake and would not have allowed anyone to break through the wall of his house.

Therefore, you too must stand ready because the Son of man is coming at an hour you do not expect.

 LOVE 10

PARABLE OF THE CONSCIENTIOUS STEWARD

`Who, then, is the wise and trustworthy servant whom the master placed over his household to give them their food at the proper time?

Blessed that servant if his master's arrival finds him doing exactly that.

In truth I tell you, he will put him in charge of everything he owns.

But if the servant is dishonest and says to himself, `My master is taking his time,'

And sets about beating his fellow servants and eating and drinking with drunkards,

His master will come on a day he does not expect and at an hour he does not know.

The master will cut him off and send him to the same fate as the hypocrites, where there will be weeping and grinding of teeth."

`Then the kingdom of Heaven will be like this: Ten wedding attendants took their lamps and went to meet the bridegroom.

Five of them were foolish and five were sensible:

The foolish ones, though they took their lamps, took no oil with them,

Whereas the sensible ones took flasks of oil as well as their lamps.

The bridegroom was late, and they all grew drowsy and fell asleep.

But at midnight there was a cry, `Look! The bridegroom! Go out and meet him.'

Then all those wedding attendants woke up and trimmed their lamps,

And the foolish ones said to the sensible ones, `Give us some of your oil: our lamps are going out.'

But they replied, `There may not be enough for us and for you; you had better go to those who sell it and buy some for yourselves.'

They had gone off to buy it when the bridegroom arrived. Those who were ready went in with him to the wedding hall and the door was closed.

The other attendants arrived later. `Lord, Lord,' they said, `open the door for us.'

But he replied, `In truth I tell you, I do not know you.'

So stay awake, because you do not know either the day or the hour.

PARABLE OF THE TALENTS

`It is like a man about to go abroad who summoned his servants and entrusted his property to them.

To one he gave five talents, to another two, to a third one, each in proportion to his ability. Then he set out on his journey.

The man who had received the five talents promptly went and traded with them and made five more.

The man who had received two made two more in the same way.

But the man who had received one went off and dug a hole in the ground and hid his master's money.

Now a long time afterwards, the master of those servants came back and went through his accounts with them.

The man who had received the five talents came forward bringing five more. `Sir,' he said, `you entrusted me with five talents; here are five more that I have made.'

His master said to him, `Well done, good and trustworthy servant; you have shown you are trustworthy in small things; I will trust you with greater; come and join in your master's happiness.'

Next the man with the two talents came forward. `Sir,' he said, `you entrusted me with two talents; here are two more that I have made.'

His master said to him, `Well done, good and trustworthy servant; you have shown you are trustworthy in small things; I will trust you with greater; come and join in your master's happiness.'

Last came forward the man who had the single talent. `Sir,' said he, `I had heard you were a hard man, reaping where you had not sown and gathering where you had not scattered;

So I was afraid, and I went off and hid your talent in the ground. Here it is; it was yours, you have it back.'

But his master answered him, `You wicked and lazy servant! So you knew that I reap where I have not sown and gather where I have not scattered?

Well then, you should have deposited my money with the bankers, and on my return I would have got my money back with interest.

So now, take the talent from him and give it to the man who has the ten talents.

For to everyone who has will be given more, and he will have more than enough; but anyone who has not, will be deprived even of what he has.

As for this good-for-nothing servant, throw him into the darkness outside, where there will be weeping and grinding of teeth.'

THE LAST JUDGEMENT

`When the Son of man comes in his glory, escorted by all the angels, then he will take his seat on his throne of glory.

All nations will be assembled before him and he will separate people one from another as the shepherd separates sheep from goats.

He will place the sheep on his right hand and the goats on his left.

Then the King will say to those on his right hand, `Come, you whom my Father has blessed, take as your heritage the kingdom prepared for you since the foundation of the world.

For I was hungry and you gave me food, I was thirsty and you gave me drink, I was a stranger and you made me welcome,

Lacking clothes and you clothed me, sick and you visited me, in prison and you came to see me.'

Then the upright will say to him in reply, `Lord, when did we see you hungry and feed you, or thirsty and give you drink?

When did we see you a stranger and make you welcome, lacking clothes and clothe you?

When did we find you sick or in prison and go to see you?'

And the King will answer, `In truth I tell you, in so far as you did this to one of the least of these brothers of mine, you did it to me.'

Then he will say to those on his left hand, `Go away from me, with your curse upon you, to the eternal fire prepared for the devil and his angels.

For I was hungry and you never gave me food, I was thirsty and you never gave me anything to drink,

I was a stranger and you never made me welcome, lacking clothes and you never clothed me, sick and in prison and you never visited me.'

Then it will be their turn to ask, `Lord, when did we see you hungry or thirsty, a stranger or lacking clothes, sick or in prison, and did not come to your help?'

Then he will answer, `In truth I tell you, in so far as you neglected to do this to one of the least of these, you neglected to do it to me.'

And they will go away to eternal punishment, and the upright to eternal life."

Jesus had now finished all he wanted to say, and he told his disciples,

`It will be Passover, as you know, in two days' time, and the Son of man will be handed over to be crucified."

But Jesus noticed this and said, "Why are you upsetting the woman? What she has done for me is indeed a good work!

You have the poor with you always, but you will not always have me. When she poured this ointment on my body, she did it to prepare me for burial.

In truth I tell you, wherever in all the world this gospel is proclaimed, what she has done will be told as well, in remembrance of her."

Now on the first day of Unleavened Bread the disciples came to Jesus to say, "Where do you want us to make the preparations for you to eat the Passover?"

He said, "Go to a certain man in the city and say to him, `The Master says: My time is near. It is at your house that I am keeping Passover with my disciples.' "

And while they were eating he said, "In truth I tell you, one of you is about to betray me."

They were greatly distressed and started asking him in turn, "Not me, Lord, surely?"

He answered, "Someone who has dipped his hand into the dish with me will betray me.

The Son of man is going to his fate, as the scriptures say he will, but alas for that man by whom the Son of man is betrayed! Better for that man if he had never been born!"

Judas, who was to betray him, asked in his turn, "Not me, Rabbi, surely?" Jesus answered, "It is you who say it."

LOVE 11

THE INSTITUTION OF THE EUCHARIST

Now as they were eating, Jesus took bread, and when he had said the blessing he broke it and gave it to the disciples. "Take it and eat," he said, "this is my body."

Then he took a cup, and when he had given thanks he handed it to them saying, "Drink from this, all of you,

For this is my blood, the blood of the covenant, poured out for many for the forgiveness of sins.

From now on, I tell you, I shall never again drink wine until the day I drink the new wine with you in the kingdom of my Father."

PETER'S DENIAL FORETOLD

After the psalms had been sung they left for the Mount of Olives.

Then Jesus said to them, "You will all fall away from me tonight, for the scripture says: I shall strike the shepherd and the sheep of the flock will be scattered,

But after my resurrection I shall go ahead of you to Galilee."

At this, Peter said to him, "Even if all fall away from you, I will never fall away."

Jesus answered him, "In truth I tell you, this very night, before the cock crows, you will have disowned me three times."

Peter said to him, "Even if I have to die with you, I will never disown you." And all the disciples said the same.

GETHSEMANE

Then Jesus came with them to a plot of land called Gethsemane; and he said to his disciples, "Stay here while I go over there to pray."

Then he said to them, "My soul is sorrowful to the point of death. Wait here and stay awake with me."

And going on a little further he fell on his face and prayed. "My Father," he said, "if it is possible, let this cup pass me by. Nevertheless, let it be as you, not I, would have it."

He came back to the disciples and found them sleeping, and he said to Peter, "So you had not the strength to stay awake with me for one hour?

Stay awake, and pray not to be put to the test. The spirit is willing enough, but human nature is weak."

Again, a second time, he went away and prayed: "My Father," he said, "if this cup cannot pass by, but I must drink it, your will be done!"

And he came back again and found them sleeping, their eyes were so heavy.

Leaving them there, he went away again and prayed for the third time, repeating the same words.

Then he came back to the disciples and said to them, "You can sleep on now and have your rest. Look, the hour has come when the Son of man is to be betrayed into the hands of sinners.

Get up! Let us go! Look, my betrayer is not far away."

So he went up to Jesus at once and said, "Greetings, Rabbi," and kissed him.

Jesus said to him, "My friend, do what you are here for." Then they came forward, seized Jesus and arrested him.

And suddenly, one of the followers of Jesus grasped his sword and drew it; he struck the high priest's servant and cut off his ear.

Jesus then said, "Put your sword back, for all who draw the sword will die by the sword.

Or do you think that I cannot appeal to my Father, who would promptly send more than twelve legions of angels to my defense?

But then, how would the scriptures be fulfilled that say this is the way it must be?"

It was at this time that Jesus said to the crowds, "Am I a bandit, that you had to set out to capture me with swords and clubs? I sat teaching in the Temple day after day and you never laid a hand on me."

Jesus answered him, "It is you who say it. But, I tell you that from this time onward you will see the Son of man seated at the right hand of the Power and coming on the clouds of heaven."

And Peter remembered what Jesus had said, "Before the cock crows you will have disowned me three times." And he went outside and wept bitterly.

And about the ninth hour, Jesus cried out in a loud voice, `Eli, eli, lama sabachthani?" that is, `My God, my God, why have you forsaken me?"

But Jesus, again crying out in a loud voice, yielded up his spirit.

And suddenly, the veil of the Sanctuary was torn in two from top to bottom, the earth quaked, the rocks were split,

The tombs opened and the bodies of many holy people rose from the dead,

And these, after his resurrection, came out of the tombs, entered the holy city and appeared to a number of people.

The centurion, together with the others guarding Jesus, had seen the earthquake and all that was taking place, and they were terrified and said, "In truth this man was son of God."

And many women were there, watching from a distance, the same women who had followed Jesus from Galilee and looked after him.

Among them were Mary of Magdala, Mary the mother of James and Joseph, and the mother of Zebedee's sons.

But the angel spoke; and he said to the women, "There is no need for you to be afraid. I know you are looking for Jesus, who was crucified.

He is not here, for he has risen, as he said he would. Come and see the place where he lay,

Then go quickly and tell his disciples, 'He has risen from the dead and now he is going ahead of you to Galilee; that is where you will see him.' Look! I have told you."

Filled with awe and great joy the women came quickly away from the tomb and ran to tell his disciples.

APPEARANCE TO THE WOMEN

And suddenly, coming to meet them, was Jesus. "Greetings," he said. And the women came up to him and, clasping his feet, they did him homage.

Then Jesus said to them, "Do not be afraid; go and tell my brothers that they must leave for Galilee; there they will see me."

Jesus came up and spoke to them. He said, "All authority in heaven and on earth has been given to me."

Go, therefore, make disciples of all nations; baptize them in the name of the Father and of the Son and of the Holy Spirit,

And teach them to observe all the commands I gave you. And look, I am with you always; yes, to the end of time."

Chunkilogy

ON MUTUAL RESPECT:

Whoever asks you to verbally "trust" them will usually be the first to betray you; truly nice and sincere people will wait and see you reveal your heart through your actions.

Everyone likes to hear that they're the best, even if they're the worst, so, nine times out of ten, if you want something bad enough in life from someone, just tell someone that at whatever they're doing, they're the best, they may not help you that day, but they'll always remember you, and possibly help you out later on in life, never burn your bridges.

In Christian purism, no sin is greater or less than any other; they are all equal, and men and women are held equally accountable. So be wary of people who put any one gender, race, person etc. on a pedestal, for they have shown you their tragic flaw, and more than likely will betray you because of it as well.

Treat everyone as equals and hold them all to the same standard, and you will be respected much more by all who encounter you.

Mutual respect for all beings, plus, you never know who's watching you, so be nice and respectful to them, if you don't know how, seek help.

Be wary of the person who expects long answers from you, yet gives you short ones in return, unless they're in extenuating circumstances. Think, are they really giving you mutual respect, ponder it again, and if not, then make the proper personal adjustments in your life.

One of the pitfalls of having mutual respect for others is having the strength, patience, and open-mindedness to meet new people for the first time and giving everyone a one time, open shot, right in your mouth, whether they throw it, mentally or physically. Then, being strong enough to pick yourself back up, and meeting the next person you meet with the same welcome. This constitutes true spiritual strength and mutual respect for all, but to do that, your personal belief system has to be unshakeable, if you're all ego and arrogance, then your facade will crumble in front of others in due time.

ON SEXUAL MATTERS:

Achieving an orgasm for women is 99% mental, 1% physical, and vice-versa for men, 1% mental, and 99% physical.

49

Let's face it, most people are bad lovers, and bad sex is more contagious than the common cold. That's why mankind invented divorce so they can try to find someone compatible the second or more times around.

If you end up having an orgasm in the exact same physical spot where you started having sex, barring environmental circumstances (i.e. hot tubs, movie theatres, etc . . .), then you, my friend, are more than likely a bad and unimaginative lover. But if both parties are happy with that all the time (never assume, ask your sexual partner), and they're happy with that, then congratulations.

ON THE TRUE NATURE OF UNCONDITIONAL LOVE:

Love everyone, never hate anyone (dislike is allowable), but stay clear of "perfect" people.

One of the biggest lessons in life is that you can love someone, but not like them or be able to grow with them, and in that case, you will probably end up initiating the process of letting them go, because sometimes that's the price of true love.

If you want to be special to anyone, listen to him or her, and then make yourself useful however they need it without getting in their way or hampering them.

Even if you have to punch out someone on the outside for being crummy, never stop loving them on the inside. And if this happens to be your significant other though, than afterwards, you should still love them enough to let them go for their own physical safety at the least. Deal with your own mental/spiritual issues by yourself, with friends, a punching bag, or with professional counseling, but get healed for the sake of mankind. Abusive love is contagious as well.

HOMOSEXUALITY:

Christ never condemned homosexuality/bisexuality personally while he walked amongst us here on Earth, nor will I, nor should mankind. Understand and/or accept people and things the way that they are, or research about them in a book or spend time walking in their shoes if you want to find out, don't ostracize and judge. Knowledge and experiences are abundant in this day and age. And if you have to pay for it, then it's a service and not love.

ON INTIMATE RELATIONSHIPS:

A healthy marriage is 99% trust, and 1% love (they trust you as a best friend, trust you to pay attention to them and make them feel special, trust you take care of your marital responsibilities, etc . . . :)

50

No matter how messed up you think you are, someone on this planet will find you irresistible, but if you know you're crummy, do you really want to be with the person(s) attracted to you in that state of mind, usually sent regards of the "Cheap & Easy" or the "Evil Sensei's" mind.

Most people don't love sex all the time, they just like it sometimes. So if you're a person that loves sex, don't marry a person that just likes it, you're asking for trouble early on in the relationship.

ON EGO/PRIDE/PERFECT PEOPLE/SELF-RIGHTEOUSNESS/CLIQUES:

Stay away from "perfect" people, they are like human scorpions, they'll sting you anyway, expect no consequences, then sting you again while asking how you how their sting felt. If you hang around them after they sting you, then that means that you accept and revel in their perfection.

In choosing friends, I prefer friends that keep their word over friends who are honest and self-righteous, in the name of their self-righteousness they'll rationale betraying you, no matter what the consequences will be to you. Then, they'll live with their regrets, and enjoy the spoils of life you leave them. Choose your friends wisely.

Be wary of ambitious people, they're set to manipulate other people's ideas and dreams and take over them for their own selfish purposes, unless you're ambitious as well and that is what you are looking for.

Never be proud, or say that you neither're proud of something, nor ask someone if they're proud, what you really mean is that you're thankful for your blessing, pride is a sin that kills.

Always strive to be happy, special, and unique. Even spiritually dead people like to be around vivacious, self-actualized people, but, if you make the choice to be spiritually dead, then don't sabotage the spiritually vivacious people in your circle, take accountability for your choice in life and live with it.

In my journeys, I've found that the most self righteous people with the biggest egos on the planet usually work for the judicial system world-wide, for to be able to judge and prosecute mankind according to the laws of man, you have to subconsciously believe that you're your own God and can pass judgement on people, I am not God nor can never guess the cosmic mind of God, so I can only pray that those people will be awakened sooner than later.

If someone doesn't like the way you eat your food in public, turn your chair around and keep eating. If they were truly your friend, non-judgmental and concerned, they would have asked, "Are you happy eating in such a manner?" if they don't, then they revealed their crummy, self-idolizing nature to you, so be wary of them.

ON DATING:

Bringing sex into a relationship, or intimate love, shouldn't change the nature of the friendship, but somehow, it always does.

When dating, keep a clear mind and heart, don't expect anything, and don't be obsessed. The perfect person goes on dates with pre-conceived expectations and usually ends up disappointed with, in their minds, the other person, but realistically, their own pre-conceived and unrealistic set of standards they brought with them on their date.

When you meet a person, and they brag about themselves dating a certain kind, type, group, race, ethnicity exclusively, don't expect deep, open-minded discussions or happy, well-balanced child-raising skills coming from this person, you already know that your relationship is going to have serious problems.

ON THE MEANING OF LIFE:

The meaning of life, if there is such a thing, is to be happy. Unfortunately, most people settle for less or compromise, and then try to achieve a simulated form of happiness for the rest of their lives, many times, based on the crushing of other people's dreams and aspirations around them.

Never pray for victory, itself, for that is a prayer to the "Adversary", pray only to the "Supreme Being" that you or your family be blessed to perform to the best of your abilities.

Try 100%, expects nothing, and appreciate everything, this way; you'll always live with no regrets.

Only a hypocrite expects the best, when they're not at their best.

ON FEELING LIKE A WINNER:

Life doesn't owe you anything; so stop demanding it from the Creator and people around you.

Whenever you help someone, it should be from the heart and you should expect nothing in return. That way, you won't be disappointed if nothing comes of it. If you can't afford to give, then don't. There's nothing wrong with that either so don't feel bad about it. If you truly can't and the person is sincere and true, but if they're tricksters, then leave them to their own devices.

Fight to step back, spiritually, from all conflicts you encounter in life, and look at everything from the big picture, situational awareness is key, and maybe life saving as well.

Good days and bad days usually come in 24-hour cycles.

Christ never specified that the Earth was the only place God created life on, so if aliens show up one day, you shouldn't lose your faith in true Christianity, Don't panic.

ON KNOW-IT-ALLS/INTELLECTUALS/SMART PEOPLE:

Be non-judgmental and let the Supreme Being be the final judge, this is true, but that doesn't mean that you have to hang around the perfect people, the world is big enough for you to stay away from them by making wise decisions in your life.

ON SPIRITUALITY/PERSONAL PEACE OF MIND:

It's hard to plan for the future when you're starving right now, mentally, physically, spiritually or emotionally. Make the proper personal adjustments in your life if you're unhappy living as such.

If someone accuses you of something that you did not do or haven't been contemplating in your mind, past or present, then you shouldn't get upset, yes?

Never believe in man-made systems, religious, socioeconomic, or in people themselves.

Don't place too much faith in people that grow up in phases, but in people that continue to grow continuously throughout their lifetimes, the latter is planted on more solid ground mentally and spiritually and they make truer friends.

Before you go to sleep every night, make sure that everyone you love or care about knows exactly how you feel, you will sleep better.

I can't move mountains, only landscape it and fly over it.

One of the other hardest lessons of life is saying "no" to the nonsense and not feeling bad about it, get over it, it's OK.

Don't take yourself seriously. We're not and will never be that important, if you can't laugh at yourself, or with others about yourself, then spiritually, you're in serious trouble and possibly in for an "Awakening"

Most of the majority is crummy, and use love or sex as a weapon of control, for their definition of love is to control the lives of the people they love, whether they're worthy of the love of the person they're trying to control or not, that possibility never enters their minds. They're never to blame, so get away from them first, and then try to help them from a distance if it's possible, after trying 100% and your "friendship" doesn't improve, then understand, accept, and let them go while you grow stronger in the purest sense of love.

53

In life, to maintain minimum minimum personal happiness, you have to have 1 of the major 3 importants in your life,

1. Live in the place you want to live.

2. Be surrounded by "true' people you love locally.

3. Be doing the thing you want to do
If you have none of these things, then you will never achieve happiness until you do something to at least attain one of the big three importants in your life. You will be miserable inside and taint all who come in contact with you.

Once someone you speak to crosses their arms or eyes, their mind closes as well, so don't waste your breath any further and walk away from the confrontation if you can, or if that's physically impossible. Take a deep breath, exhale, and let it go. If it is a recurring problem, then seek other, more congenial ways to peacefully solve it, maybe even by convincing them that they came up with your peaceful solution to make their egos feel better, perhaps?

ON FINANCIAL MATTERS:

Money won't buy you love, but it'll buy you a darn good substitute.

ON TRADITIONAL CHRISTIANITY

There is no more Sabbath.

We don't know the actual date of Christ's birth or resurrection, so celebrate for the memory of it, but don't swear by it, modern XMAS should be everyday.

The church is flesh now, you and me following Christ's teachings and living Christ-like, which means on the streets and out and about, not imposing Evil Sensei teachings on others and suckering the young and lost Majority into buildings the Evil Sensei's deemed "churches", so if you're in a building every week, calling it a church/temple/synagogue", and hanging in self-righteous cliques, you're not following Christ's teachings, don't kid yourself about it.

The "Genesis" tale originated in Babylon, and was written while the Jews were in Babylon for the Old Testament.

There's still a ban on graven images for religious/spiritual purposes, i.e., crosses and so forth. Christ didn't endorse any of it.

Paul was a good disciple, but he is not Christ, and I'm a Christian Purist, and believe in the words and teaching of Christ alone, good luck in your buildings and cliques. **I don't believe in Paul, I believe in Christ alone** so stop quoting him as if he were a deity that should have that amount of significance to me.

If I'm getting the reader angry, then, my apologies for having hurt your comfortable belief system. And if you're lost or in the in-between and I'm confusing you, good, now do some homework on your own if you're truly concerned about your religion.

CLONING

Clones are made by using a small part of the life force of another living being and nurturing it into a mature living being. This is the same as life force stored in the reproductive genes of a mature living being, humans included. Therefore, once the clone seed is put in a nurturing environment, like an infant being, the new human infant clone, like a human infant, will have its own soul. "Cloners" (people who make clones) can thereby be considered as, "soul-makers". And it's the cloner's responsibility, being its parents, to raise, nurture, and teach the clone just like the natural born human child. Their responsibility should not and does not end with the human clone birth process alone.

ANIMAL SLAVERY

Adopt a human child please, stop adopting these animals and treating them better than your fellow human brothers and sisters. Either eat the animals or let them be. Too many humans get mauled by "friendly" pets every year or go to the hospitals for allergy shots that would have kept a human child alive. Set them all free. Thanks for reading and sharing.

* Glossary section

SEXUAL CANNIBALISM -
When a group of people hangs around each other for any length of time
in hopes eventually having sex with each and every other member of that
particular group or clique

PERFECT PEOPLE -
Hypocrites, self-righteous, inventors of man-made systems to snag the
lazy, content majority, they and all in their clique are going to their
pre-conceived notion of the afterlife according to the misguiding and
selfish teachings of their own prospective perfect people leader(s)

CHEAP & EASY -
Going for what is immediately in front of you thoughtlessly without
contemplating the repercussions

SUPREME BEING/LIFE-FORCE/GOD/ALLAH/CHI/CREATOR -
whatever you call the Creator of/or life force

MAJORITY -
Over 90% of the masses that are open to some level of spiritual
connection with the Creator

ADVERSARY -
Satan, Beelzebub, Mephistopheles, Hades, selfish nature of mankind,

AWAKENING -
The point/time in most of the lives of the majority, when they realize,
without the help of mankind, but on their own, that their total trust
in the man-made system they were raised/trained in is mostly bull-shit
(and that life/the universe/the Earth) don't revolve around them

THE "LIE" -
Man-made systems, belief, physical, or otherwise

EVIL SENSES -
The demagogue leaders of the majority who, once they figure that
they're losing you from the Majority, will send all forms of physical
temptations to you in attempts to bring you back into the fold of the
lost Majority

THE 3 IMPORTANTS -
#1 - live in the place you want to live,
#2 - be surrounded by "true" people you love locally,
#3 - or be doing the thing you want to do

57

58

ABOUT THE AUTHOR

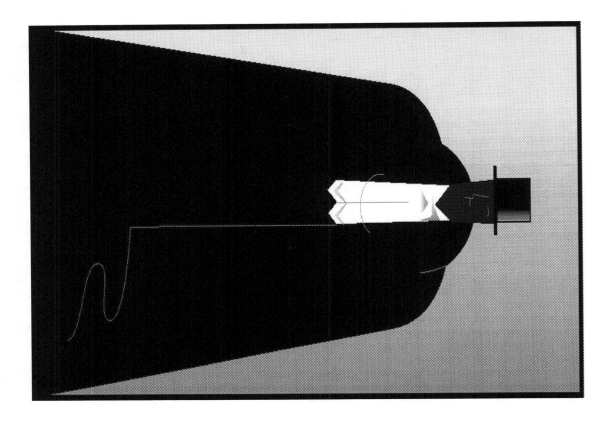

Chun Ki was last spotted . . .